はじめに

　本書は、高校生及び高等専門学校の学生（高専生）を対象に、高専生の日常生活が題材の英会話を中心としたリスニング力とスピーキング力を高めるためのテキストです。英語を使うことに慣れ親しんでいない学生たちにとって、英語でコミュニケーションを取ることには少なからず不安や抵抗があるかもしれません。しかし、言語はコミュニケーションの手段であり、使いこなせるようになれば、学びの楽しさや自信を感じることができるはずです。本書では、学生たちが無理なく英語を身につけ、実際の会話の中で自分の意見や考えを表現できるようになることを目標として編集されています。

　工学において「サーキット」は電気が流れる道筋を指します。エネルギーが部品間を巡るように、コミュニケーションも話し手と聞き手の間を行き交う言葉によって成り立ちます。サーキットが光を灯すように、適切な言葉のやり取りによって新たな気づきや理解が生まれます。そのためには、語彙・文法・発音・流暢さといった要素が結びつき、絶えず循環することが不可欠です。学生たちにとって、英語のスピーキング力は国際的なネットワークへとつながる鍵です。サーキットと同様に、明確で精密、かつダイナミックな構造が求められます。楽しく英語でコミュニケーションをとることで、心のなかの明かりが次々と灯されてゆき、それが自信へとつながることを願っています。

　さらに、テキスト後半にはTOEIC Bridge® 対策としてリスニングテストを2回分収録しています。これにより、実際の試験形式に触れることができ、リスニング力を強化することができます。

　なお、本書編集にあたり、非常に有能なイラストレーターや音声のスペシャリストに恵まれました。本編のイラストはMaro氏、音声プロダクションそして表紙デザインはBunkasha Internationalのグラフィックデザイナーと動画編集者であるMarko Ćošković氏、TOEICのイラストは本校美術科講師の奈須ゆかり氏に参画いただきました。この場をお借りして、心から感謝申し上げます。

　そして末筆ですが、本書出版の契機を与えてくださった株式会社大学教育出版の佐藤守社長と編集部の皆様に心から御礼申し上げます。

2025年4月

編著者一同

目次　CONTENTS

はじめに･･･ 1
本書の構成と学習のねらい･･ 3
登場人物紹介･･･ 4
学生のための教室英語･･･ 5

CHAPTER ❶	COLLEGE LIFE　（高専生活）･･････････････････････････････	7
CHAPTER ❷	LEISURE TIME　（余暇時間）･･････････････････････････････	12
CHAPTER ❸	FAMILY & FRIENDS　（家族・友人）････････････････････････	17
CHAPTER ❹	DIRECTIONS & PLACES　（方向・通学）････････････････････	22
CHAPTER ❺	LUNCH TIME　（昼休み・食事）････････････････････････････	27
CHAPTER ❻	HEALTH CENTER　（保健室・健康）････････････････････････	32
CHAPTER ❼	COMPETITIONS　（コンテスト）･･･････････････････････････	37
CHAPTER ❽	FESTIVALS & EVENTS　（祭り・学園祭）･･････････････････	42
CHAPTER ❾	SAFETY DRILL　（防災訓練）･････････････････････････････	47
CHAPTER ❿	VACATIONS　（長期休暇）････････････････････････････････	52
CHAPTER ⓫	VOLUNTEERING　（ボランティア活動）･････････････････････	57
CHAPTER ⓬	CULTURAL EXCHANGE　（文化交流）･･････････････････････	62

TOEIC　Bridge®　リスニングテスト ①　──────────────── 67
TOEIC　Bridge®　リスニングテスト ②　──────────────── 71

☑ 音声ファイルについて

音源は大学教育出版が提供する次の URL からダウンロードします。
https://www.kyoiku.co.jp/06support/circuit.html

※ CHAPTER の 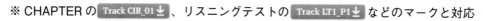、リスニングテストの などのマークと対応

本書の構成と学習のねらい

本書は、高等専門学校の学生および「高専」の生活について学びたい1年生を対象とした英語の教科書です。12のCHAPTERは6人の学生の日常生活を題材に、後半に向かって段階的に難易度を上げた構成になっています。これにより、学生は無理なく、基礎から応用まで英語力を高めることができます。

各CHAPTERは、以下の6つのセクションで構成されています。これらのセクションを通して、学生は英語の4技能（聞く、話す、読む、書く）をバランス良く学習できます。

📌 各セクションの詳細と学習効果

Warming Up
短いリスニング練習で背景知識を確認し、ペアワークで自由に意見交換することでスピーキングへの抵抗感を減らし、積極性を促します。

Conversation
空欄補充でリスニング力を強化し、ロールプレイで学んだ語彙や表現を実際に使う練習をします。

Expressions
ミニダイアログを通して実際の会話での語彙の使い方を学び、下線部を置き換える練習で表現力を高めます。

Presentation
プレゼンテーションを通して、構成力、表現力、発表力を総合的に高めます。学生が自分の意見を発表することに対して自信をつけます。

Reading
音声を聞きながら文章を読み、リスニング力と読解力を向上させます。T/F問題で理解度を確認します。

Self-Check
理解度を確認する質問に答えることで学習内容を整理し、ペアワークでさらに理解を深めます。

📌 凡例 ― 各Chapter「Reading」における単語の品詞略号

v	verb 動詞	ger	gerund 動名詞	art	article 冠詞
n	noun 名詞	adv	adverb 副詞	prep	preposition 前置詞
pron	pronoun 代名詞	adj	adjective 形容詞	p.p.	past participle 過去分詞

📌 アイコンの意味

 Speaking 話す   Writing 書く   Listening 聴く   Reading 読む   Reviewing 復習する

📌 TOEIC Bridge® リスニングテスト対策と学習の進め方

本書には、TOEIC Bridge®対策として、2つのリスニングテストが収録されています。各テストは4つのパートで構成され、実際の試験形式に慣れることを目標にしています。

CHARACTER PROFILES
登場人物紹介

1年5組
1st year group 5

TAKUMI
- **Club:** Robot Technology
- **Interested in:** AI
- **Personality:** Quiet and analytical
- **Activities:** Playing video games and watching YouTube

AIKA
- **Club:** English (president)
- **Interested in:** Cybersecurity
- **Personality:** Organized and ambitious
- **Activities:** Learning about foreign cultures

MISAKI
- **Club:** Volleyball (captain)
- **Interested in:** Electronics
- **Personality:** Hardworking and responsible
- **Activities:** Spending time in nature and volunteering

HARUTO
- **Club:** English
- **Interested in:** Machine maintenance
- **Personality:** Reliable and thoughtful
- **Activities:** Visiting historical sites

KOHEI
- **Club:** Baseball (pitcher)
- **Interested in:** Manufacturing
- **Personality:** Friendly and cheerful
- **Activities:** Playing sports and eating delicious food

RENA
- **Club:** English & Student Council
- **Interested in:** Architecture
- **Personality:** Calm and gentle
- **Activities:** Designing and making handmade crafts

Classroom English for Students
学生のための教室英語

Teacher's instructions（先生の指示）

Sit down / Take a seat.	座ってください
Stand up.	立ってください
Raise your hand.	手を挙げてください
Listen (carefully).	（よく）聞いてください
Listen and repeat.	聞いて繰り返してください
Read aloud.	音読してください
Answer the question(s).	質問に答えてください
Who would like to start? / Who would like to be the first?	最初に発表したい人はいますか？
Be quiet, please.	静かにしてください
Work in pairs.	2人1組で課題をやってください
Work in groups.	グループで課題をやってください
Open your books to page「52」.	「52」ページを開いてください
Write this down.	これを書き留めてください
Speak up.	声を出してください
Say it in English / In English, please.	英語で言ってください
Put your「tablets」away.	「タブレット」をしまってください

Clarification, asking for help（説明・明確）

Can you repeat, please?	もう一度言ってください
I'm sorry, I don't know.	すみません、知りません
I'm sorry, I don't understand.	すみません、分かりません／理解できません
I'm sorry, I didn't hear. / I'm sorry I didn't catch that.	すみません、聞こえませんでした
I'm sorry, I don't remember.	すみません、覚えていません
What does「activities」mean?	「activities」とはどういう意味ですか？
How do you say「*bukatsu*」in English?	「部活」は英語で何と言いますか？
Could you explain again?	もう一度説明してもらえますか？
May I ask a question? / I have a question.	質問してもいいですか？

Other（その他）

I'm sorry, I'm late.	遅くなってすみません
May I come in?	入ってもいいですか？
Can I borrow your「pencil」, please?	「鉛筆」を借りてもいいですか？
May I go to the bathroom, please?	お手洗いに行ってもいいですか？
I'm sorry, I forgot to bring my「homework」.	すみません、「宿題」を持ってくるのを忘れました
Can I bring it to your office?	オフィスに持って行ってもいいですか？
I'm sorry I feel sleepy today.	すみません、今日は眠いです
I don't feel well today.	今日は、あまり気分が良くありません

■写真提供■

Chapter 2_ p. 14　Tima Miroshnichenko | PEXELS
Chapter 3_ p. 19　takasu | イメージマート
Chapter 6_ p. 34　buritora | Adobe Stock
Chapter 10_ p. 54　yasuyasu99 | Adobe Stock
Chapter 12_ p. 62　maxfromhell | iStock by Getty Images

CHAPTER ① COLLEGE LIFE

- 📌 **Topic**: Talking about life at a technical college
- 📌 **Interaction**: "What club are you in?"
- 📌 **Presentation**: "Nice to meet you"

Warming Up

Listen and fill in the blanks. Then, write your own answers and practice asking and answering the questions with your partner. Track CIR_01

1. What time do you wake up on weekdays?
   —I wake up at _____ on weekdays.
2. How long does it take you to get to college?
   —It takes me about _____ .
3. How many classes do you have per week?
   —I have over _____ classes a week.
4. Do you spend more time studying or hanging out with friends?
   —I spend more time _____ .

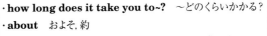
- **how long does it take you to~?** ～どのくらいかかる？
- **about** およそ, 約
- **spend time**+動詞-ing ～することに時間を費やす

Expressions

A *Practice each dialogue with your partner. Memorize new expressions.*

1. A: **What do you want to study at a technical college?**
   B: I want to study <u>programming</u>. / I'm interested in <u>mechanics</u>.
2. A: **What is the most difficult subject for you?**
   B: <u>Physics</u> is the most difficult subject. / I'm not good at <u>English</u>.
3. A: **Are you in any college clubs or societies?**
   B: Yes, I'm in <u>the baseball club</u>. /
   No, but I'm thinking about joining <u>the student council</u>.
4. A: **What do you usually do after classes?**
   B: Usually, <u>I go home</u> and <u>do my homework</u>.

Technical college 高専
- **general subjects** 一般科目 ▶ math 数学, physics 物理, chemistry 化学, English 英語, geography 地理, history 歴史, social studies 社会, physical education 体育, art 美術
- **technical subjects** 専門科目 ▶ engineering 工学, programming プログラミング, mechanics 機械工学, designing デザイン, information 情報, robotics ロボット, technology 技術, architecture 建築学, electricity 電気, electronics 電子, AI
- **clubs** 部活 ▶ light music 軽音部, brass band 吹奏楽部, motorsports モータースポーツ部, baseball 野球部, track and field 陸上部, student council 学生会, go-home club 帰宅部

B *Replace the underlined words with your own variants and practice again.*

Reading

A *Listen to the audio while reading the text. Check the new words below.* Track CIR_02

📍 *Kosen* lifestyle

Have you ever heard of *kosen*? *Kosen* is a technical college in Japan where students can study things like engineering, electronics, and computers. Students can enter *kosen* after finishing junior high school and study there for five years.

At technical colleges, students do not just study from books; they also work on real projects. For example, they build robots, design machines, or make computer programs.

Life at a technical college is busy. Classes usually start around 9:00 a.m. and finish in the late afternoon. But there is also time for fun! Many students join clubs—some enjoy sports, others play music, and some do art.

Learning how to manage time is important at *kosen*. Students need to balance their studies, club activities, and free time. This not only makes them more responsible but also prepares them for future work.

---

    adj   n   n prep   n
technical college (college of technology)
工業高等専門学校（高専）
  v
enter 入学する
   adj   adj   n
junior high school 中学校
  adj   n
real project 実践的なプロジェクト
 v
build 製作する
  prep
around 頃
 v   n
join (club) クラブに参加する

     v   n
manage (time) 時間を管理する
    v
balance バランスを取る
       adj
responsible 責任ある
    v
prepare 備える

> ※「**not only [A], but also [B]**」は、2つのアイテムやアクションなどを強調するために使われる構文。「AだけでなくBも…」と表現される。

B *True or False. Find the evidence in the text.*

1. Students can start studying at *kosen* after junior high school. [TRUE / FALSE]
2. *Kosen* students have flexible schedules. [TRUE / FALSE]
3. There is no time for fun at technical colleges; students only study. [TRUE / FALSE]
4. Learning time management positively affects students. [TRUE / FALSE]

Conversation

A *Listen to the conversation. Fill in the gaps with words you hear (find them in the word box below). Be careful! There are extra words in the word box.* Track CIR_03

sport	computers	before	junior high	activities	study	cool	volleyball
soft tennis	programming	homework	baseball	societies	building	after
robotics	three times	doing	elementary	technology

🔑 What club are you in?

Takumi: What do you do ₁_____ classes, Misaki?
Misaki: Usually, I go home and do my ₂_____ . But today I have club ₃_____ .
Takumi: Oh, really? What club are you in?
Misaki: I'm in the ₄_____ club. We practice ₅_____ a week.
Takumi: I see! How long have you been practicing?
Misaki: Since ₆_____ school.
Takumi: That's impressive! You must be pretty good at it by now.
Misaki: How about you? Are you in any college clubs or ₇_____ ?
Takumi: No, but I'm thinking about joining the ₈_____ club.
Misaki: That sounds ₉_____ ! Do you love ₁₀_____ things?
Takumi: Very much!

B *Group work. Use the above dialogue as a model and make your own conversation about your club activities.*

Presentation

Complete the short self-presentation paragraph by filling in your own information. Use new expressions you have learned. Memorize it!

Nice to meet you

Hello! My name is _____(名前). Everyone calls me _____(ニックネーム). I'm _____(年齢) years old. I'm from _____(出身).

I'm a _____(学年) year student at _____(高専名). Let me tell you about my college life. I wake up at _____(時間) every day. It takes me about _____(何分・何時間) to get ready in the morning. Then, I go to college. It takes me about _____(何分・何時間) to get to the campus. I have _____(クラス数(トータル)) classes per week. My favorite class is _____(科目名), but I don't like _____(科目名) because _____(理由). In the future, I want to study _____(専門科目).

After classes, I usually _____(放課後にすること). I'm in the _____(クラブ名) club. I practice/we meet _____(週に何回) (times) a week.

My hobby is _____(趣味). I like _____(趣味) because _____(理由).

Nice to meet you!

10

Self-Check

Let's see how well you understood the topic! Answer the following questions based on the chapter. If you are not sure, review the chapter to help you.

1. Can you explain what "kosen" is?
   _____.

2. What are some technical subjects students can study at *kosen*?
   _____.

3. How many classes do first-year college students usually have per week?
   _____.

4. What time do classes start and finish at *your* college?
   _____.

5. What are some fun activities students can do after classes?
   _____.

6. What clubs can students join at *your* college?
   _____.

7. Why is time management important for college students?
   _____.

8. What is your favorite thing about *kosen* lifestyle?
   _____.

9. What is the most difficult part of life at *kosen*?
   _____.

10. Do you think it's more important to study or hang out with friends at college?
    _____.

CHAPTER ② LEISURE TIME

- 📌 **Topic**: Talking about free time
- 📌 **Interaction**: "Do you have any plans later?"
- 📌 **Presentation**: "My weekends"

Warming Up

Listen and fill in the blanks. Then, write your own answers and practice asking and answering the questions with your partner.

1. Which do you like better, quiet weekends or busy weekends?
   —I like _____ weekends better.
2. Which do you prefer, planning your free time or being spontaneous?
   —I prefer _____.
3. Would you rather stay at home or go out with your friends?
   —I'd rather _____.
4. When do you do your homework, on weekends or on weekdays?
   —I usually do my homework on _____.

> · **which do you like better/ prefer: [A] or [B]~**
> 〜[A]と[B]、どっちの方が好き？
> ＊名詞又は動名詞 (-ing形)
> · **would you rather [A] or [B]~**
> 〜[A]と[B]、どっちがいい？
> ＊動詞の原形
> · **spontaneous** 自発的に

Expressions

A *Practice each dialogue with your partner. Memorize new expressions.*

1. A: **Do you have a lot of free time?**
   B: Yes, I do. / No, I don't. Because <u>I have a lot of homework</u>.
2. A: **Which do you prefer: passive or active leisure activities?**
   B: I prefer <u>passive leisure activities</u>. I like <u>reading</u>.
3. A: **How did you spend your last weekend?**
   B: I <u>played computer games</u> and <u>munched on snacks</u> all day.
4. A: **What are you planning to do next weekend?**
   B: I'm planning to <u>go shopping with my friends</u>. /
   I'm not sure yet, but maybe <u>I'll stay home and clean my room</u>.

> Leisure activities　余暇活動
> · **passive**　受動的▶ reading 読書, sleeping 睡眠, watching TV テレビを見る, listening to music 音楽を聴く, playing video games ビデオゲームをする, browsing the internet ネットサーフィン, munching on snacks スナックをむしゃむしゃ食べる
> · **active**　能動的▶ riding bicycle 自転車に乗る, jogging ジョギング, swimming 水泳, hiking ハイキング, playing/doing sports スポーツをする, making handmade things 手作りする, cleaning 掃除する, going shopping ショッピングに行く

B *Replace the underlined words with your own variants and practice again.*

Reading

A *Listen to the audio while reading the text. Check the new words below.* Track CIR_05

📍 College students' leisure time

In Japan, college students enjoy their free time in many different ways. Some spend all their free time doing club activities.

But a lot of students like to hang out with friends off-campus. They often meet at cafés, shopping centers, or karaoke to chat and have fun together. This helps them to take a break from their studies and relax.

Some students also enjoy cultural activities like tea ceremonies or calligraphy. Others prefer outdoor activities, like hiking in the mountains, fishing, or visiting shrines. Playing video games is another popular pastime. Many young people love gaming on their consoles or smartphones.

Finally, some use their leisure time to learn new skills like cooking or photography, while others enjoy hobbies like collecting things or watching movies.

How about you? How do you usually spend your free time?

---

leisure time 余暇時間 (n n)
off-campus 学外で (adv)
chat おしゃべり，歓談 (n)
a break from 〜からの休憩 (art n prep)
cultural activities 文化活動 (adj n)
tea ceremony 茶道 (n n)

calligraphy 書道 (n)
outdoor activities 野外活動 (adj n)
pastime 娯楽 (n)
console ゲーム機 (n)
finally 最後に，また (adv)

※「**some~, while others~**」「〜もいれば、〜もいる」、物事を対比する際によく使われる。

B *True or False. Find the evidence in the text.*

1. College students hate going out with friends in their free time. [TRUE / FALSE]
2. Cultural activities include calligraphy, tea ceremonies, and video games. [TRUE / FALSE]
3. Outdoor activities are as popular as indoor activities. [TRUE / FALSE]
4. Leisure time can be used to enjoy hobbies. [TRUE / FALSE]

Conversation

A *Listen to the conversation. Fill in the gaps with words you hear (find them in the word box below). Be careful! There are <u>extra</u> words in the word box.* Track CIR_06

fun	chat	karaoke	basketball	study	alone	relax	active
exercise	café	do sports	time	break	off-campus	video games
shop	together	munch	read	passive

Do you have any plans later?

Takumi: I'm so tired today, I need a ₁_____ from studying.
Kohei: Me too. Do you have any plans later?
Takumi: Hmm, there's no club meeting today. Maybe I'll just play ₂_____ at home.
Kohei: What about you, Misaki?
Misaki: I was planning to go to the library to ₃_____ . Why do you ask?
Kohei: Let's do something ₄_____ after classes! Maybe something ₅_____ ?
Misaki: Like what?
Kohei: How about playing ₆_____ ?
Takumi: Oh, I don't really want to ₇_____ today...
Misaki: Then why don't we go to that new ₈_____ near the train station? They have delicious desserts.
Kohei: Sounds great! We can ₉_____ and ₁₀_____ there. What do you think, Takumi?
Takumi: Sure, I'm up for it.

B *Group work. Use the above dialogue as a model and make your own conversation about your plans after school.*

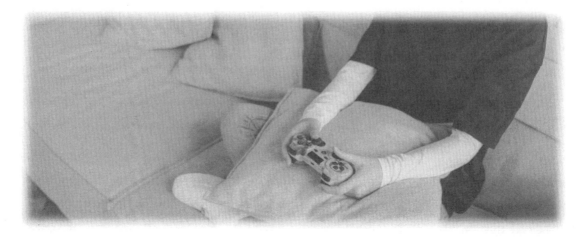

14

Presentation

Complete the short presentation paragraph by filling in your own information. Use new expressions you have learned. Memorize it!

My weekends

Let me tell you how I spend my weekends. My weekends are usually busy/quiet.

On Saturday and Sunday, I wake up at _____ (何時に) o'clock. On weekdays, I usually sleep for _____ (何時間) hours. But when I don't have school, I sleep for _____ (何時間) hours.

After waking up, I have a nice breakfast. Then, I usually enjoy my free time. I prefer active/passive leisure activities. I often _____ (アクティビティ1), _____ (アクティビティ2), or _____ (アクティビティ3) on weekends.

In the evening, I usually _____ (夕方の行動1) or _____ (夕方の行動2).

On Sunday, after breakfast, I _____ (午前は何をする) in the morning, and then I _____ (午後は何をする). Sometimes, I go to _____ (屋外活動) with my family/friends.

Before going to bed, I _____ (寝る前の行動1) and _____ (寝る前の行動2).

On Monday, I feel _____ (気分) and ready/not ready for the new week.

This is what my weekends look like!

Self-Check

Let's see how well you understood the topic! Answer the following questions based on the chapter. If you are not sure, review the chapter.

1. Can you explain what "leisure time" is?

   _____.

2. What are examples of passive leisure activities?

   _____.

3. What are examples of active leisure activities?

   _____.

4. What cultural activities can students do in their free time?

   _____.

5. What are the most popular leisure activities among students in *your* college?

   _____.

6. What are popular places for students in *your* college to hang out off-campus?

   _____.

7. Do you think doing club activities on campus is "free time"? Why or why not?

   _____.

8. Is it better to plan your free time or be spontaneous? Why?

   _____.

9. Do you think free time is more enjoyable when you are alone or with friends? Why?

   _____.

10. What is the best way to take a break from studying, in your opinion?

    _____.

CHAPTER 3
FAMILY & FRIENDS

- 📌 **Topic**: Talking about people in your life
- 📌 **Interaction**: "Do you have strict parents?"
- 📌 **Presentation**: "My best friend"

Warming Up

Listen and fill in the blanks. Then, write your own answers and practice asking and answering the questions with your partner.

1. Do you live with your family or in a dormitory?
   —I live _____.
2. Who usually helps you with your homework?
   —My _____ usually helps me with my homework.
3. Who do you usually ask for advice: friends or family?
   —Usually, I ask my _____ for advice.
4. Do your parents get angry if you get a bad grade, or do they support you?
   —My parents _____ if I get a bad grade.

- **dormitory** 寮
- **ask for advice** 助言を求める
- **get angry** 怒る
- **grade** 成績

Expressions

A *Practice each dialogue with your partner. Memorize new expressions.*

1. **A: How many friends do you have?**
   B: I have <u>five</u> friends. Most of them are <u>guys</u>.
2. **A: Can you tell me about your best friend?**
   B: Well, <u>she</u> is <u>very kind</u> but <u>a little short-tempered</u>.
3. **A: Do you make friends easily?**
   B: Yes, I do, because <u>I like talking to new people</u>. /
   No, I don't. <u>I'm a little shy</u>.
4. **A: How often do you hang out with your friends?**
   B: Usually, we hang out <u>twice a week, on weekends</u>.

Personality traits 性格特性
- **positive** 肯定的 ▶ friendly 友好的, kind 優しい, smart 賢い, honest 正直, supportive 応援してくれる, reliable 信頼できる, cheerful 明るい, optimistic 前向き, hardworking 勤勉な, responsible 責任のある, understanding 物分かりの良い
- **neutral** 中立 ▶ easygoing のんびり屋, shy 恥ずかしがり屋, talkative おしゃべり, quiet 静かな, serious まじめ, independent 独立した, strict 厳しい
- **negative** 否定的 ▶ boring つまらない, lazy 怠け者, forgetful 忘れっぽい, short-tempered 短気, pessimistic 悲観的, demanding 気むずかしい, stubborn 頑固な

B *Replace the underlined words with your own variants and practice again.*

Reading

A *Listen to the audio while reading the text. Check the new words below.* Track CIR_08

Living with family or in a dormitory?

When Japanese students start college, they have two options: living in a dormitory or staying with their parents. Each choice gives a different experience.

Living in a dormitory helps students become more independent and make new friends. It is easier to join social activities and learn important skills like solving problems, managing time, and sharing space with others. But dormitories can be noisy and expensive. There is little privacy, and living with roommates can sometimes be challenging.

Staying with parents is more comfortable and cheaper. Students do not need to pay for rent or food. Family can also give emotional support. But living at home can stop students from becoming independent because they might depend too much on their families.

Both choices have good and bad sides. Which one would you choose?

---

v **start** 入学する	n **privacy** プライバシー、内密
n **experience** 経験	adj **challenging** 困難なこと
adj n **social activities** 社会活動	n **rent** 家賃
ger n **solving problem** 問題を解決する	v n **give support** 支援を与える
n **roommate** 同居人	adj **independent** 独立
	v prep **depend on** 〜に頼る

B *True or False. Find the evidence in the text.*

1. Living in a dormitory can help college students become more responsible. [TRUE / FALSE]
2. Dormitories have a lot of privacy. [TRUE / FALSE]
3. Living with parents costs more than staying in a dormitory. [TRUE / FALSE]
4. Students living with their families can get help and support from their parents. [TRUE / FALSE]

Conversation

A *Listen to the conversation. Fill in the gaps with words you hear (find them in the word box below). Be careful! There are extra words in the word box.* Track CIR_09

kind	serious	laid-back	shy	sad	short-tempered	independent
demanding	irresponsible	pessimistic	stubborn	lazy	hardworking
smart	supportive	relaxed	easy-going	noisy	optimistic	strict

Do you have strict parents?

Takumi: What's wrong Kohei? You look upset.

Kohei: I got my math exam grade, and it's not good. I don't know how to tell my parents.

Misaki: Do you have ₁_____ parents?

Kohei: I do. They are very ₂_____ when it comes to grades.

Takumi: Are your parents the same, Misaki?

Misaki: Not really. They are pretty ₃_____. They think being ₄_____ is important, so I manage my studies myself.

Kohei: That's because you are a ₅_____ and ₆_____ student.

Takumi: My dad is ₇_____, but my mom can be ₈_____. She says I'm ₉_____ ...

Misaki: Anyway, Kohei, what will you do?

Kohei: I don't know... If I tell them, they will get angry for sure.

Misaki: Oh, don't be so ₁₀_____! It's not the end of the world.

B *Group work. Use the above dialogue as a model and make your own conversation about your parents.*

Presentation

Complete the short presentation paragraph by filling in your own information. Use new expressions you have learned. Memorize it!

My best friend

Let me tell you about my best friend. His/Her name is _____ [友人の氏名]. He/She is _____ [年齢] old.

He/She lives near/far away from me in _____ [どの都市で、家族と、あるいは寮に].

We met _____ [何年・何ヶ月] ago _____ [どこ]. We quickly/slowly became best friends.

_____ [友人の名前] is a very _____ [性格のよいところ1], and _____ [性格のよいところ2] person, but sometimes he/she can be a bit _____ [性格の欠点1] and _____ [性格の欠点2]. I also like him/her because _____ [親友を好きな具体的な理由].

_____ [友人の名前] 's hobby is _____ [友人の趣味], I think he/she is very good at it.

I'm happy when we spend time together. We usually hang out _____ [回数] a week. Last time we _____ [前回、一緒に行ったこと].

In the future, _____ [友人の名前] wants to become a/an _____ [職業・仕事]. Doesn't that sound _____ [形容詞（かっこいい、凄い、怖い等）]?

I want us to be best friends forever!

Self-Check

Let's see how well you understood the topic! Answer the following questions based on the chapter. If you are not sure, review the chapter.

1. Does *your* college have a dormitory? How many students live there?
   _____.

2. What are some challenges students face when living in a dormitory?
   _____.

3. What are some benefits of living with family while studying?
   _____.

4. In your opinion, what personality traits make a roommate easy to live with?
   _____.

5. Can you give an example of a problem a student might have with a roommate?
   _____.

6. Do you think good grades are the result of being smart or hardworking?
   _____.

7. Do you think strict parents make students more responsible? Why?
   _____.

8. How does your family react if you get a bad grade?
   _____.

9. What personality traits can help a student make friends easily?
   _____.

10. Is it better to have many friends or just a few close friends? Why?
    _____.

CHAPTER ④
DIRECTIONS & PLACES

- **Topic**: Getting around campus and the city
- **Interaction**: "Let's choose the club meeting place"
- **Presentation**: "My favorite place in town"

Warming Up

Listen and fill in the blanks. Then, write your own answers and practice asking and answering the questions with your partner. Track CIR_10

1. Is it easier to get to the campus by bus or on foot?
   —It's easier to get to the campus _____ .
2. How long does it take to get from your house to downtown?
   —It takes about _____ to get downtown.
3. Which is closer to your classroom, the library or the cafeteria?
   —The _____ is closer.
4. What is the nearest train station to your house?
   —The nearest station to my house is _____ station.

> - **is it easier to [A] or [B]?**
>   ～[A]と[B]ではどちらが簡単ですか？
>   *動詞の原形
> - **to get from [A] to [B]**
>   ～[A]から[B]に移動する
> - **downtown** 中心街
> - **library** 図書館
> - **cafeteria** 食堂
> - **nearest** 最寄りの（最上級の形容詞）

Expressions

A *Practice each dialogue with your partner. Memorize new expressions.*

1. A: **How do you get to college every day?**
   B: I take the train and then walk for 20 minutes.
2. A: **Can you tell me how to get to the cafeteria?**
   B: Sure! Go straight and turn left at the second building. The cafeteria is across from the library.
3. A: **How far is the gym from the main entrance?**
   B: It's about a 5-minute walk from the main entrance.
4. A: **Where is the best place to study on campus?**
   B: The best place to study is in the student lounge.

> **Getting around 移動**
> - **moving** 移動▶ **take**: バス、電車、タクシーなどの公共交通機関（public transportation）を利用するときに使う。**ride**: 「またがる」タイプの乗り物が基本だが、バスや電車でも使うことがある。**go**: 目的地への移動全般を表す。交通手段は "by" や "on" で指定する。
> - **directions** 道順▶ go straight まっすぐ行く、turn right/left 右/左に曲がる、go along ～に沿って行く、turn around 振り向く、cross the road 道を渡る、go past 通り過ぎる
> - **positions** 位置▶ in front of ～の前、behind ～の後ろ、across from ～の向かい側、next to ～の隣、near ～の近く、between ～の間、around the corner 角を曲がったところ、on the left/right 左/右側に

B *Replace the underlined words with your own variants and practice again.*

Reading

A *Listen to the audio while reading the text. Check the new words below.* `Track CIR_11`

📍 Train, bus, or bike? Commuting to college in Japan

In Japan, commuting to and from college is a big part of students' daily routine. The average travel time is about 45 minutes each way.

Some students take the train if they live far away. To save money, many buy a commuter pass. For students without a nearby train station, the bus is a good option. Dormitory students often use a special shuttle bus that goes straight to campus, which is very convenient. Others ride bicycles or walk if they live close by. This is a good exercise and helps them save money.

However, when the campus is in a remote area, students often need to make several transfers. In this case, there is no time to spare—if you miss your ride, you might have to walk or wait for the next one.

How do you usually commute to college?

---

commute/commuting (v/ger) 通学する
daily routine (adj/n) 日常生活，毎日の習慣
average (adj) 平均的な
save money (v/n) 節約する
commuter pass (adj/n) 定期券（通勤・通学）
nearby (adj) 最寄りの
shuttle bus (n/n) 送迎バス
straight to (adv/prep) 直行する
convenient (adj) 便利な

close by (adj/adv) 近くに
several (adj) いくつかの，複数
remote (adj) 遠隔
transfer (n) 乗り換え
miss (v) 遅れる
ride (v) 乗る（バス）

※「**in this case, ~**」(prep/pron/n)「この場合〜」
※「**no time to spare**」(adj/n/prep/v)「暇がない，時間に余裕がない」

B *True or False. Find the evidence in the text.*

1. The average travel time to college in Japan is less than one hour.   [TRUE / FALSE]
2. All students in Japan use public transportation to get to school.   [TRUE / FALSE]
3. A commuter pass helps students spend less on travel.   [TRUE / FALSE]
4. If a student misses their ride, they can skip classes that day.   [TRUE / FALSE]

Conversation

A *Listen to the conversation. Fill in the gaps with words you hear (find them in the word box below). Be careful! There are extra words in the word box.* Track CIR_12

in front of	cafeteria	parking	principal	volunteer	gym	second
between	next to	light music	Student Council	designing	lounge
brass	Building 2	behind	third	across from	main entrance	nearby

📍 Let's choose the club meeting place

Aika: Okay, we need to decide where to have English club meetings this year.
Haruto: What's wrong with the room in ₁_____ the club used last year?
Rena: The ₂_____ band will be practicing on the sports ground ₃_____ it. It'll be too noisy!
Haruto: Oh, I see. How about Kosen Hall? There's a ₄_____ there.
Aika: It's already taken by the ₅_____ group.
Rena: There's a library ₆_____ Kosen Hall. Maybe we could use the ₇_____ floor?
Aika: It closes at 3:00 PM...
Haruto: That's too early.
Rena: Wait, what about Building 1? It's ₈_____ the library and Building 4, near the bicycle ₉_____.
There are two big rooms with projectors.
Haruto: Sounds good! Can we reserve one of those rooms?
Aika: Let's check with the ₁₀_____.

B *Group work. Use the above dialogue as a model and make your own conversation about choosing a club meeting place.*

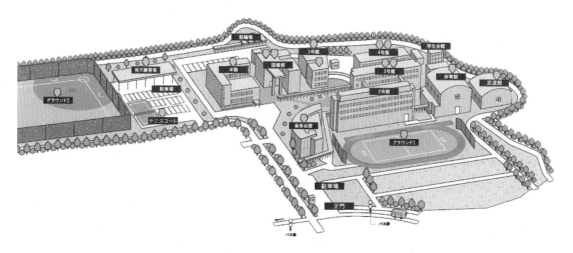

Presentation

Complete the short presentation paragraph by filling in your own information. Use new expressions you have learned. Memorize it!

My favorite place in town

Let me tell you about my favorite place in _____[市町村名または都道府県名]_____. It's _____[地名]_____.

_____[地名]_____ is located in _____[どこにあるのか]_____. I go there _____[頻度]_____ to _____[行く目的1]_____ and _____[行く目的2]_____.

I first visited _____[地名]_____ _____[初めてそこに行ったとき（いつ）]_____, and since then, it has become my favorite spot in the city. It's a perfect place for _____[アクティビティ1]_____, _____[アクティビティ2]_____, or _____[アクティビティ3]_____.

To get there from _____[出発地]_____, take a/the _____[交通手段]_____ and get off at _____[降りる所]_____. From there, it's a (short) _____[何分]_____ walk to _____[地名]_____.

Last time, I went to _____[地名]_____ I _____[何をしました]_____.

It's my favorite place because it always makes me feel _____[どんな気持ちになるか1]_____ and _____[どんな気持ちになるか2]_____.

I recommend you visit _____[地名]_____ when you have time.

Self-Check

Let's see how well you understood the topic! Answer the following questions based on the chapter. If you are not sure, review the chapter.

1. What does "to commute" mean?

   _____.

2. What are some ways students can save money on commuting to college?

   _____.

3. What is the average commuting time for students in *your* college?

   _____.

4. How do students usually commute to *your* college?

   _____.

5. How far is *your* campus from the nearest train station?

   _____.

6. What do students in *your* college do to pass the time during their commute?

   _____.

7. What are the main buildings on *your* campus?

   _____.

8. Which campus building do you visit most often? How do you get there from the main gate?

   _____.

9. How do students in *your* college decide where to meet for club activities?

   _____.

10. What do you usually do if you miss your ride/forget your commuter pass?

    _____.

CHAPTER ⑤
LUNCH TIME

- 📌 **Topic**: Discussing eating habits
- 📌 **Interaction**: "What's today's special?"
- 📌 **Presentation**: "My daily diet"

Warming Up

Listen and fill in the blanks. Then, write your own answers and practice asking and answering the questions with your partner.

1. Do you eat lunch in the cafeteria or bring a lunch box?
   —I usually _____.
2. Is making lunch at home cheaper or more expensive than buying it?
   —I think making lunch at home is _____.
3. Which has more calories: a rice ball or a hamburger?
   —I think _____ has more calories.
4. Which is the healthiest snack: an apple, a bag of chips, or yoghurt?
   —I think _____ is the healthiest snack.

> - **lunch box** お弁当
> - **calories** カロリー
> - **rice ball** おにぎり
> - **which/what/who has more [N]: [A] or [B]?**
>   [A]と[B]、どちらのほうが[N]が多い？

Expressions

A *Practice each dialogue with your partner. Memorize new expressions.*

1. A: **How many meals do you have per day?**
   B: I have <u>four</u> meals a day: <u>breakfast, lunch, dinner, and a snack</u>.
2. A: **Are there any foods you dislike?**
   B: I don't like the <u>taste of eggs</u>. / I'm not a big fan of <u>spicy food</u>.
3. A: **Do you have any food allergies?**
   B: Yes, I'm allergic to <u>mushrooms</u>. / I have a <u>nut</u> allergy. /
      No, I'm not allergic to any foods.
4. A: **Do you count calories when you eat?**
   B: Yes, I do. / No, I don't, but I try to eat <u>small portions</u>.

> **Eating** 食生活
> - **meals** 食事 ▶ breakfast 朝食, lunch 昼食, brunch ブランチ, dinner 夕食, snack 軽食, supper 夜食
> - **food** 食べ物 ▶ healthy 健康的, unhealthy 不健康的, organic 有機食品, fresh 新鮮, fatty 脂っこい, salty しょっぱい, light あっさりした, heavy 胃にもたれる, spicy 辛い, vegetarian 菜食主義の
> - **eating habits** 食習慣 ▶ have an allergy/be allergic to ～にアレルギーがある, keep to a diet ダイエットする, count calories カロリーを計算する
> - **other** 関連語彙 ▶ dish 料理, portion 分量, ingredient 材料, taste 味, diet 食生活

B *Replace the underlined words with your own variants and practice again.*

Reading

A *Listen to the audio while reading the text. Check the new words below.*

📍 Eating at the cafeteria or bringing a lunch box?

Lunchtime is often the best part of the day for many college students. When the bell rings, students quickly split into two main groups: those who rush to the cafeteria and those who look for a nice spot to eat their packed lunch.

Eating at the cafeteria is convenient. Students can choose from different meals, like a rice bowl with tasty toppings, warm or cold noodles, and fresh salads. There are desserts, too. If you're really hungry, you can ask for a bigger portion. The food is served quickly, and there's no need to wash dishes afterward.

Bringing a lunch box is another good option. Students can prepare their favorite foods at home, which is great for people with allergies or those who count calories. There's no waiting in line, which means more time to enjoy your meal. Plus, making lunch at home can save money.

Do you eat lunch at the cafeteria or bring a lunch box?

---

n
bell チャイム
v
split 分かれる
v
rush 急ぐ
v prep
look for 探す
 adj   n   n   n
packed lunch/lunch box 弁当
n
meal 食事
n   n
rice bowl 丼
 n
topping 上に乗せるもの，ふりかけ

n
noodles 麺
n
dessert デザート
v
serve 提供する
adv
afterward その後
prep n
 in line 列に
v   n
save (money) （お金を）節約する。

※「**choose from ~**」「~から選ぶ」、複数の選択肢の中から一つを選ぶときに使う。

B *True or False. Find the evidence in the text.*

1. During a lunch break, students usually go home to eat.   [TRUE / FALSE]
2. Students can enjoy desserts after their meals in the cafeteria.   [TRUE / FALSE]
3. A packed lunch is a good option for students with special eating habits.   [TRUE / FALSE]
4. Eating in the cafeteria costs the same as bringing a lunch box.   [TRUE / FALSE]

Conversation

A *Listen to the conversation. Fill in the gaps with words you hear (find them in the word box below). Be careful! There are extra words in the word box.* Track CIR_15

dessert	portion	snacks	wait	count calories	miso soup
dishes	menu	cake	light	lunch box	options	rush	plate
udon noodles	rice bowl	salad	topping	line	keep to a diet

What's today's special?

Kohei: Finally, a lunch break! I'm so hungry... Oh no! I forgot my ₁_____ at home!

Haruto: Let's eat at the cafeteria then. I always eat there.

Kohei: Okay, let's hurry up! There's always a ₂_____ . in the cafeteria

Kohei: Wow, there are so many ₃_____ ! What are you going to get?

Haruto: Hmm, the chicken-and-egg ₄_____ looks delicious.

Kohei: But look, it says it's sold out.

Haruto: That's too bad. Then I will have warm ₅_____ . What about you?

Kohei: I'm really hungry, so I need a big ₆_____ . What's today's special?

Haruto: Stir-fried pork with soy sauce. It comes with a ₇_____ and ₈_____ on the side.

Kohei: Sounds good! I'll have that. Should we get a ₉_____ too?

Haruto: Actually, I'm trying to ₁₀_____ , so I'll skip it.

B *Group work. Use the above dialogue as a model and make your own conversation about lunchtime.*

Presentation

Complete the short presentation paragraph by filling in your own information. Use new expressions you have learned. Memorize it!

My daily diet

Let me tell you about my eating habits. I think I have a/an unhealthy/healthy daily diet. I eat ___(何食)___ main meals a day: ___(1食目)___, ___(2食目)___, and ___(3食目)___. In the morning, I'm usually (not) very hungry, so I eat ___(食べる物1)___ and ___(食べる物2)___ for breakfast. I like to drink ___(飲み物)___ with my breakfast.

On weekdays, I eat lunch at college. I always pack my lunchbox/go to the cafeteria. For lunch, I often have ___(食べる物1)___, ___(食べる物2)___, and sometimes ___(食べる物3)___.

I eat dinner with my family at home/with my friends at the dormitory. For dinner, I usually eat ___(食べる物1)___, ___(食べる物2)___, or ___(食べる物3)___. I enjoy snacks like ___(軽食1)___ and ___(軽食2)___.

I'm allergic to ___(アレルギー食品)___, so I avoid it. / I don't have food allergies, so I can eat everything. I don't like ___(嫌いな食べる物)___ because ___(理由)___. Usually, I (don't) count calories, and I eat small/big portions.

This is what my daily diet looks like.

Self-Check

Let's see how well you understood the topic! Answer the following questions based on the chapter. If you are not sure, review the chapter.

1. What is a "packed lunch," and what can you put in it?

   _____.

2. What are the benefits of eating in the cafeteria?

   _____.

3. What are the benefits of bringing a lunch box?

   _____.

4. What are the menu options at the cafeteria in *your* college?

   _____.

5. Do you think food at the cafeteria is expensive or cheap?

   _____.

6. Do most students in *your* group bring lunch or eat in the cafeteria?

   _____.

7. What do you think is the healthiest lunch option for students? Why?

   _____.

8. What is your favorite meal of the day, and why?

   _____.

9. Do you think eating snacks during the day is healthy or unhealthy? Why?

   _____.

10. If you had to eat the same lunch every day in college, what meal would you choose and why?

    _____.

CHAPTER ⑥
HEALTH CENTER

- 📌 **Topic**: Talking about health
- 📌 **Interaction**: "You should go to the nurse's office"
- 📌 **Presentation**: "How I stay healthy"

Warming Up

Listen and fill in the blanks. Then, write your own answers and practice asking and answering the questions with your partner. **Track CIR_16**

1. How many hours do you usually sleep at night?
   —I usually sleep about _____ to _____ hours a night.
2. Do you feel tired or refreshed when you get up in the morning?
   —I usually feel _____ when I get up in the morning.
3. Do you stay at home or go to school if you have a cold?
   —I _____ if I have a cold.
4. Do you feel like sleeping or drinking coffee when you're tired?
   —I feel like _____ when I'm tired.

- **refreshed** すっきりした
- **cold** 風邪
- **feel like**＋動詞-ing
  〜したい気分である，〜したいと思う

Expressions

A *Practice each dialogue with your partner. Memorize new expressions.*

1. A: **How do you feel today?**
   B: I feel great. / I feel <u>unwell</u>. I <u>have a headache</u>.
2. A: **What do you do when you <u>catch a cold</u>?**
   B: I <u>drink hot tea</u>, <u>take medicine</u>, and <u>sleep</u>.
3. A: **How do you stay healthy?**
   B: I <u>eat fruits and vegetables</u> and <u>go for a walk</u> <u>every day</u>. /
   I don't do anything special to stay healthy.
4. A: **How often do you go to the <u>doctor</u>?**
   B: I usually go to the <u>doctor</u> <u>once a year</u>.

Health 健康
- **have** 症状▶ a headache 頭痛, a stomachache 腹痛, a sore throat のどの痛み, a fever 熱
- **feel** 感じる▶ sick/unwell 具合が悪い, dizzy めまいがする, weak 弱っている, tired 疲れている
- **catch** かかる▶ a cold 風邪をひく, a virus ウイルスに感染する
- **break** 骨折する▶ a leg 足, an arm 腕, a bone 骨
- **take** 取る▶ medicine 薬を飲む, vitamins ビタミンを取る, a rest 休憩する
- **go to the** 行く▶ nurse's office 保健室, doctor 医者, hospital 病院

B *Replace the underlined words with your own variants and practice again.*

Reading

A *Listen to the audio while reading the text. Check the new words below.*

📍 Visiting the Health Center

There are different names for the place where students go when they don't feel well, such as the *health room*, *nurse's office*, or *infirmary*. Many colleges in Japan have Health Centers on campus to help students stay healthy.

If you feel dizzy, have a headache, or have a small injury, you can visit the Health Center for first aid, health advice, and check-ups. The nurse will check your temperature, ask about your symptoms, and may give you over-the-counter medicine. Health Centers usually have beds where you can take a short nap to feel refreshed. However, for serious problems, like a broken bone, students are sent to the hospital.

Some Health Centers have counseling rooms where students can talk about their feelings. Counselors help students with stress and other mental health concerns.

How often do you visit the Health Center at your college?

---

n n **Health Center** 保健室, 保健管理センター	adj n **over-the-counter (OTC) medicine** 処方箋不要の医薬品
n **nurse** 看護師	v art adj n **take a (short) nap** 仮眠を取る
n **infirmary** 診療所	adj n **broken bone** 骨折
n **injury** 怪我	n n **counseling room** 相談室
adj n **first aid** 応急手当て, 救急療法	n **counselor** 相談員
n **check-up** 健康診断	n **feelings** 気持ち
n **temperature** 温度	adj n **mental health** 心の健康
n **symptom** 症状	n **concern** 悩み

B *True or False. Find the evidence in the text.*

1. If you feel dizzy after gym class, you can rest in the Health Center. [TRUE / FALSE]
2. The nurse always gives medicine to students who feel unwell. [TRUE / FALSE]
3. Students with serious health problems must stay in the Health Center all day. [TRUE / FALSE]
4. If students feel stressed, they can talk to a counselor in the counseling room. [TRUE / FALSE]

Conversation

A *Listen to the conversation. Fill in the gaps with words you hear (find them in the word box below). Be careful! There are extra words in the word box.* `Track CIR_18`

sick	better	sleep	weak	stomachache	Health Center	vitamins
virus	symptoms	going home	dizzy	healthy	cold	temperature
headache	infirmary	taking a nap	size	OTC medicine	rest	

You should go to the nurse's office

Aika: Hey, Takumi, are you okay? You don't look well.

Takumi: No, I'm not. I have a ₁_____, and I feel very tired. I felt ₂_____ in gym class, and now it's worse.

Aika: Oh, your ₃_____ don't sound good! You should go to the nurse's office. Maybe you're getting ₄_____.

Takumi: Yeah, maybe. But I have an important class after the break. I don't want to miss it.

Aika: It's better to take care of your health first. The nurse can check your ₅_____. You might have a fever and need to ₆_____.

Takumi: You're right. I feel like ₇_____. I'll go to the ₈_____ now.

Aika: Good idea! The nurse might give you some ₉_____, too.

Takumi: Thanks for the advice. I'll go now.

Aika: I hope you feel ₁₀_____ soon!

B *Group work. Use the above dialogue as a model and make your own conversation about visiting a Health Centre.*

Presentation

Complete the short presentation paragraph by filling in your own information. Use new expressions you have learned. Memorize it!

How I stay healthy

It's important to take care of myself, so I do a few things every day to stay healthy.

First, I make sure to get enough sleep. I usually sleep for _____ (何時間) hours every night. If I don't get enough sleep, I feel _____ (気分) the next day.

Second, it is important to eat healthy food. I try to eat _____ (食べる物1) , _____ (食べる物2) , and _____ (食べる物3) every day. Eating healthy food gives me the energy to _____ (何をする1) and _____ (何をする2) .

I also exercise/play sports _____ (頻度) times a week. / I usually don't exercise because _____ (理由) .

When I feel sick, I usually _____ (何をする1) and _____ (何をする2) .

Finally, to stay mentally healthy, I _____ (心の健康のためにすること1) and _____ (心の健康のためにすること2) . I _____ (ストレスを感じたとき何をする) when I feel stressed. It helps me relax.

Staying healthy is important because it helps me _____ (健康でいることがなぜ重要なのか) and enjoy my daily life.

Self-Check

Let's see how well you understood the topic! Answer the following questions based on the chapter. If you are not sure, review the chapter.

1. What are other names for the "Health Center"?

   _____.

2. When can students visit the Health Center?

   _____.

3. What can the nurse at the Health Center help you with?

   _____.

4. What are counseling rooms at colleges used for?

   _____.

5. How often do you visit the Health Center at *your* college?

   _____.

6. What was the reason for your last visit to the Health Center?

   _____.

7. What are some common symptoms of a cold?

   _____.

8. Should students stay home when they are sick or still come to classes? Why?

   _____.

9. What are some healthy habits students can follow to avoid getting sick?

   _____.

10. What do you usually do to relax when you feel stressed?

    _____.

CHAPTER ⑦ COMPETITIONS

- 📌 **Topic**: Participating in college contests
- 📌 **Interaction**: "We made it to the All-Japan Tournament"
- 📌 **Presentation**: "A challenge I overcame"

Warming Up

Listen and fill in the blanks. Then, write your own answers and practice asking and answering the questions with your partner. **Track CIR_19**

1. Which type of contests do you like: sports, technology, or art?
   —I like _____ competitions.
2. What do you enjoy more: watching or participating in sports competitions?
   —I enjoy _____ sports competitions more.
3. Do you prefer being a team player or competing on your own?
   —I prefer _____ .
4. What is more important in a competition: winning or having fun?
   —I think _____ is more important.

- **type of**　～の種類
- **participate**　～に参加する
- **team player**　チームプレーヤー
- **compete**　競争する
- **on your own**　一人で

Expressions

A *Practice each dialogue with your partner. Memorize new expressions.*

1. A: **Have you ever participated in a contest?**
   B: Yes, I have. I participated in a <u>speech contest</u> <u>last year</u>. /
   　 No, I have never participated in a contest.
2. A: **What kind of contests are popular at your college?**
   B: <u>Sports competitions</u> are the most popular.
3. A: **Did the <u>ROBOCON</u> team make it to the finals?**
   B: Yes, they did. They won <u>a trophy</u>, too! /
   　 No, they didn't. They <u>lost in the semifinals</u>.
4. A: **What is the most important thing to win a <u>baseball game</u>?**
   B: I think <u>teamwork</u> is the most important.

```
Competitions　競技大会
・participate in/take part in
　参加する ▶ a contest　コンテスト,
　a competition　競技
・win　受賞する ▶ a prize　賞,
　a medal　メダル, a trophy
　トロフィー
・lose　負ける ▶ a game/a match
　試合
・compete　競争する ▶ against a
　team　チームと, in a game　ゲー
　ムに, for a title　タイトル争い
・make it to　に進む ▶ the finals
　決勝, the tournament　トーナメント
・show　見せる ▶ teamwork　チーム
　ワーク, skills　技術, talent　才能
```

B *Replace the underlined words with your own variants and practice again.*

Reading

A *Listen to the audio while reading the text. Check the new words below.*

🔑 *Kosen* contests and tournaments

Every year, technical college students participate in various contests and tournaments where they show their skills and talents.

One of the most popular events is the Robot Contest (ROBOCON). In this contest, students build robots to complete tasks like picking up objects or moving through obstacles. They work hard to make creative robots.

In the Programming Contest (PROCON), students solve problems using computer code. Teams are judged on how fast and efficient their programs are.

Students use their engineering skills in the Design Contest (DEZACON) to suggest ideas that solve real-world problems and make life easier.

At the English Presentation Contest (PRECON), students give speeches in English on different topics. It helps them improve their speaking skills, become more confident, and prepare for a global future.

Of course, there are sports tournaments like soccer, basketball, and track and field. These events show students' physical skills, teamwork, and sportsmanship.

Are you joining any "CON" or tournaments this year?

---

tournament (n) 大会，試合
various (adj) 様々な
complete task (v)(n) 課題をこなす/完了する
object (n) 物体，モノ
moving through (ger)(prep) 通過する，越える
obstacle (n) 障害物，邪魔
creative (adj) 独創的な
solve problem (v)(n) 問題を解決する

efficient (adj) 効率的な
suggest (v) 提案する
real-world (adj) 実社会の
improve (v) 向上させる
confident (adj) 自信がある
global future (adj)(n) グローバルな将来
sportsmanship (n) スポーツマン精神

B *True or False. Find the evidence in the text.*

1. ROBOCON is one of the most popular contests at technical colleges. [TRUE / FALSE]
2. DEZACON is a contest where students practice their programming skills. [TRUE / FALSE]
3. PRECON helps students practice public speaking in English. [TRUE / FALSE]
4. The sports tournaments are only for individual athletes, not for teams. [TRUE / FALSE]

Conversation

A *Listen to the conversation. Fill in the gaps with words you hear (find them in the word box below). Be careful! There are <u>extra</u> words in the word box.* Track CIR_21

won	medal	program	group	speech	DEZACON	soccer team
presentation	single	ROBOCON	script	robot	lost	skills
baseball team	match	design	trophy	team	PROCON

We made it to the All-Japan Tournament

Takumi: Hey, did you hear? Our ₁_____ team made it to the All-Japan Tournament!

Rena: Congrats! You must be very excited!

Takumi: Yes, we worked very hard on our ₂_____ . It's clever, and the ₃_____ is cool, too.

Kohei: That's awesome! What about PRECON, Rena? Are you participating this year?

Rena: Yes, we will compete in the ₄_____ division with Haruto and Aika. It's really difficult to remember the ₅_____ , so we're practicing every day.

Kohei: Sounds tough, but I'm sure you'll do great. Good luck with the ₆_____ !

Takumi: By the way, how's the ₇_____ doing?

Kohei: We ₈_____ our last game, so we must win the next ₉_____ to go to the finals. It's going to be tough, but we're ready.

Rena: Good luck, Kohei! I'm sure you'll make it and win the ₁₀_____ .

B *Group work. Use the above dialogue as a model and make your own conversation about contests you want to take part in.*

Presentation

Complete the short presentation paragraph by filling in your own information. Use new expressions you have learned. Memorize it!

A challenge I overcame

Let me tell you about a challenge I overcame. This happened _____(いつ)_____.

It was very hard for me to/ I struggled with _____(困ったこと・挑戦・克服しなければならなかったこと)_____. At first, I felt _____(当初の気持ち)_____ and didn't know what to do.

To overcome this challenge, I decided to _____(決心したこと)_____. I practiced/trained/studied/ _____(どのような行動をとったか)_____, every day/for several weeks/ _____(頻度)_____.

The hardest part was _____(一番大変だったこと)_____, but I didn't give up. I also got support from _____(手伝ってくれた人)_____. After some time, I started to feel more _____(行動を起こした後の気持ち)_____.

In the end, I was able to _____(チャレンジの結果)_____. I learned that _____(学んだこと)_____.

Now, I feel proud of myself because I _____(なぜ自分に誇りを持っているか)_____. Overcoming this challenge showed me that I can _____(実際にできること)_____.

Now, I'm ready to face new challenges!

Self-Check

Let's see how well you understood the topic! Answer the following questions based on the chapter. If you are not sure, review the chapter.

1. What competitions can students join at technical colleges?

   _____.

2. What competitions or tournaments has *your* college won this year?

   _____.

3. Which competitions or tournaments do you think *your* college will win next?

   _____.

4. What is the most exciting competition or tournament held at *your* college?

   _____.

5. What skills can students learn by joining competitions?

   _____.

6. What do you think students can learn from losing a competition?

   _____.

7. What challenges do students face when preparing for competitions?

   _____.

8. What advice would you give to a friend who feels nervous before a competition?

   _____.

9. In your opinion, what is the biggest benefit of joining a competition?

   _____.

10. If you could create a new competition for students, what would it be?

    _____.

CHAPTER 8
FESTIVALS & EVENTS

- **Topic**: Talking about local festivals and events
- **Interaction**: "Let's write a proposal for the school fair"
- **Presentation**: "My favorite festival"

Warming Up

Listen and fill in the blanks. Then, write your own answers and practice asking and answering the questions with your partner. Track CIR_22

- **organize** 企画する
- **just** ただ
- **attend** 参加する
- **talent show** タレントショー
- **school fair** 学園祭
- **around** くらい，だいたい

1. Do you go to school festivals with your friends or with your family?
   —I usually go with _____ .
2. Do you take part in organizing school festivals, or do you just attend them?
   —I usually _____ school events .
3. Which do you like better: watching a school talent show or participating in games?
   —I like _____ better.
4. How much money do you usually spend at school fairs?
   —I usually spend around _____ yen at school fairs.

Expressions

A *Practice each dialogue with your partner. Memorize new expressions.*

1. A: **Have you ever helped organize a school fair?**
   B: Yes, I helped with <u>decorations last year</u>. /
   No, I've never helped before.
2. A: **What do you think is the most fun part of a festival?**
   B: I think <u>the game booths</u> are the most fun part.
3. A: **Would you like to perform on stage?**
   B: Yes, I would. <u>I want to perform with a light-music band</u>. /
   No, I wouldn't. <u>I'd be too nervous</u>.
4. A: **What food do you usually buy at festivals?**
   B: I usually get <u>grilled corn</u> and <u>cotton candy</u>.

School festival 学園祭
- **places** 場所▶ stage ステージ, festival ground 祭り会場, food stall 屋台, entrance gate 入口, game booth ゲームブース
- **activities** 活動▶ watch a performance パフォーマンスを見る, play games ゲームをする, listen to live music ライブ音楽を聴く, take pictures 写真を撮る, dance 踊る, eat snacks お菓子を食べる, wear a costume 衣装を着る, have fun 楽しむ
- **atmosphere** 雰囲気▶ cheerful 明るい, lively 賑やか, exciting ワクワクする, friendly 和やかな
- **festival food** 食べ物/飲み物▶ cotton candy 綿菓子, popcorn ポップコーン, fried noodles 焼きそば, grilled corn 焼きとうもろこし, lemonade レモネード, soft drinks ソフトドリンク

B *Replace the underlined words with your own variants and practice again.*

Reading

A *Listen to the audio while reading the text. Check the new words below.*

📍 Time to have fun at the school fair

In Japan, school fairs, or *bunkasai*, are one of the most exciting parts of college life. Every year, students and teachers work together to organize this special event. The planning usually starts a few months before the fair. Students work together to write a proposal, create activities, set up stalls, and decorate the campus.

The school fair usually takes place over a weekend. Both students and local people come to join the fun. There are many activities to enjoy. Some students run food stalls, selling popular festival snacks like cotton candy or grilled corn. Others perform on stage with music bands, dance groups, and even comedy shows. Some students set up game booths, like ring toss or bingo, where visitors can win small rewards.

During the fair, everyone is busy, but the hard work pays off when people arrive and enjoy the event. School fairs are great for students to show their talents, have fun, and unite the community.

---

   adj   n prep
exciting part of ～の楽しみのひとつ
  n
planning 企画，準備
  n
proposal 企画書
  v
create 作成する，創り出す
  v
set up 設置する
  v
decorate 飾り付ける，装飾する
  adj   n
local people 地元の人々
  v
run 運営する，出店する（屋台）
  v
perform 演じる，パフォーマンスを行う

  n   n
ring toss 輪投げ
  n
bingo ビンゴ大会
  n
visitor 来場者
  n
reward 褒賞
  v
unite 結びつける，団結させる
  n
community 地域社会

※「**take(s) place**」は、特定のイベントが「行われる」や「開催される」という意味の表現で、主語によって動詞の形が変わる。
※「**hard work pays off**」は、「努力が報われる」という意味のイディオム(慣用表現)。

B *True or False. Find the evidence in the text.*

1. Planning for school fairs usually starts only a week before the event.   [TRUE / FALSE]
2. Local people are welcome to join school fairs in Japan.   [TRUE / FALSE]
3. Food stalls at school festivals only sell traditional Japanese snacks.   [TRUE / FALSE]
4. Students who like music or acting often perform at school fairs.   [TRUE / FALSE]

Conversation

A *Listen to the conversation. Fill in the gaps with words you hear (find them in the word box below). Be careful! There are extra words in the word box.* Track CIR_24

art wall	rewards	getting	bingo	food stall	decorations
organize	proposal	café	game booth	plan	ring toss	stuff	dance
winning	balloon pop	karaoke contest	gifts	talent show	set up

📍 **Let's write a proposal for the school fair**

Misaki: We need to decide what to do for the school fair. Any ideas?

Haruto: How about we run a ₁_____? We could sell popcorn or fried noodles.

Aika: But we did that last year. Let's try something new. Maybe a ₂_____?

Misaki: It is a good idea, but I think a ₃_____ might bring more people.
 Everyone loves fun challenges and ₄_____ prizes.

Haruto: Yeah, and it would be easier to ₅_____ . We won't need too many things.

Aika: We could do something like a ₆_____ or darts.

Haruto: How about a ₇_____? It's simple, and we can give small
 ₈_____ to the winners.

Misaki: That's perfect! Let's go with it. I'll write the ₉_____ .

Haruto: I'll help get the ₁₀_____ for the booth.

Aika: And I will find some fun prizes for the winners. This is going to be great!

B *Group work. Use the above dialogue as a model and make your own conversation about an activity you want to propose for the school fair.*

Presentation

Complete the short presentation paragraph by filling in your own information. Use new expressions you have learned. Memorize it!

My favorite festival

Every year, I look forward to the _____祭りの名前_____ festival. It's a popular cultural/musical/food/seasonal/ _____祭りのタイプ_____ festival. It takes place in _____場所_____ in _____月・季節_____. I first went there when I was _____年齢_____.

This festival is special because _____祭りの特徴_____. The atmosphere is always _____雰囲気_____. People come to enjoy activities like _____アクティビティ1_____ and _____アクティビティ2_____.

You can also buy delicious treats from the food stalls, like _____祭りの食べ物・飲み物1_____, _____祭りの食べ物・飲み物2_____, or _____祭りの食べ物・飲み物3_____.

My favorite part of the festival is _____祭りで好きなアクティビティ_____ because _____理由_____. I usually go with my _____誰と_____. Last time, we _____思い出に残ったこと・やったこと_____, and it was a lot of fun.

I love the _____祭りの名前_____ festival and can't wait to go again! You should come too!

Self-Check

Let's see how well you understood the topic! Answer the following questions based on the chapter. If you are not sure, review the chapter.

1. Can you explain what a "school fair" is?

   _____.

2. How do students and teachers get ready for school festivals or events?

   _____.

3. What food and drinks are usually sold at school fairs?

   _____.

4. What performances can you watch at a school festival?

   _____.

5. When does *your* college hold its school fair?

   _____.

6. What do students usually wear to school festivals at *your* college?

   _____.

7. Which stalls are the most popular at *your* college's school fair?

   _____.

8. What was the atmosphere like at the last school fair you went to?

   _____.

9. What do you think is the hardest part of organizing a school fair?

   _____.

10. Why do you think local people like to visit school festivals?

    _____.

CHAPTER ⑨
SAFETY DRILL

- 📌 **Topic**: Talking about safety and sharing drill experiences
- 📌 **Interaction**: "Did anyone get hurt?"
- 📌 **Presentation**: "The time I felt scared"

Warming Up

Listen and fill in the blanks. Then, write your own answers and practice asking and answering the questions with your partner. **Track CIR_25**

1. Do you know when *Disaster Prevention Day* is in Japan?
   —Yes, it's every year on _____ .
2. How often do you have safety drills in your college?
   —We usually have them _____ .
3. Which do you feel is scarier: earthquakes or fires?
   —I think _____ are scarier.
4. What do you think is more important in an emergency: staying calm or acting quickly?
   —I think _____ is more important.

- **disaster** 災害
- **prevention** 防止
- **safety drills** 避難訓練
- **earthquake** 地震
- **fires** 火災
- **emergency** 緊急, 非常

Expressions

A *Practice each dialogue with your partner. Memorize new expressions.*

1. A: **Have you ever experienced a real emergency?**
   B: Yes, I have. It was a <u>big earthquake two years ago</u>. /
   No, luckily, I haven't been in an emergency before.
2. A: **What emergency drills are practiced at your college?**
   B: We have <u>evacuation drills</u> and <u>first aid training</u>.
3. A: **What do you always keep in your emergency kit?**
   B: I keep a <u>flashlight</u>, <u>water</u>, and a <u>first aid kit</u>.
4. A: **What do you think is the most important thing to do during an emergency?**
   B: I think the most important thing is <u>to stay calm</u> and <u>help others</u>.

Emergency 緊急関連
- **type of an emergency** 緊急事態の種類 ▶ earthquake 地震, fire 火事, typhoon 台風, flood 洪水, accident 事故, blackout 停電
- **safety drill** 安全訓練 ▶ alarm アラーム, evacuation 避難, emergency exit 非常口, assembly point 集合場所
- **emergency items** 非常用品 ▶ fire extinguisher 消火器, emergency kit 非常用キット, first aid kit 応急処置キット, flashlight 懐中電灯
- **feelings** 感情 (be/stay) ▶ scared 怖い, anxious 不安な, calm 落ち着いている, relieved 安心している, collected 冷静な, focused 集中している

B *Replace the underlined words with your own variants and practice again.*

Reading

A *Listen to the audio while reading the text. Check the new words below.* Track CIR_26

🔑 Learning to stay safe

Do you know what "duck, cover, and hold" means? It's not a funny game—it's an important earthquake safety drill. When the earthquake alarm sounds, students must quickly get under desks, cover their heads, and hold on tightly. This simple action helps avoid panic and keeps everyone safe during a quake. But it's not something people naturally know how to do, which is why safety drills are so important.

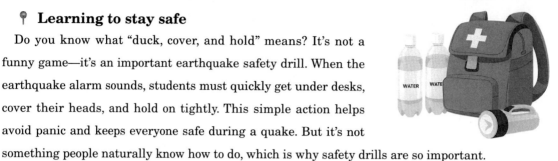

Annual safety drills in Japanese colleges include evacuation drills, fire drills, and first aid lessons. Students, teachers, and staff practice how to evacuate, use fire extinguishers, and call for help when needed. Professional firefighters and emergency workers are often invited to give instructions.

Also, since *kosen* students often work with machines and chemicals, they must be extra careful. In case of an accident, students are taught to follow safety rules, help others, and stay calm.

These drills remind everyone of the importance of being prepared. Practicing regularly teaches students how to protect themselves and others in real emergencies.

---

v
duck 身をかがめる
v
sound 鳴る
adv
tightly しっかり
v
avoid 避ける
n
quake 地震, 揺れ
adv
naturally 自然に
adj
annual 毎年の
n　　　n
emergency worker 救急隊員

n
chemicals 化学物質
adv
extra 特に
v
remind (人)に気づかせる
adv
regularly 定期的に

※「**in case of [A]~**」は「もし~の場合」「~に備えて」「~が起こったら」という意味で使われ、通例、文頭で用いられる。
※「**remind [A] of [B]**」「AにBのことを思い出させる」という意味で使われる表現。

B *True or False. Find the evidence in the text.*

1. Safety drills in Japanese colleges are practiced not only by students. [TRUE / FALSE]
2. In case of an emergency, students are instructed to panic to get attention. [TRUE / FALSE]
3. "Duck, cover, and hold" is a safety drill designed for fires. [TRUE / FALSE]
4. As a rule, safety training happens every year. [TRUE / FALSE]

Conversation

A *Listen to the conversation. Fill in the gaps with words you hear (find them in the word box below). Be careful! There are extra words in the word box.* Track CIR_27

team	alarm	escape	panicking	emergency	earthquake	relieved
assembly	shaking	department	fire	safety drills	calm	blackout
signal	evacuate	anxious	gathering	shouting	smoke	

Did anyone get hurt?

Takumi missed the classes yesterday

Rena: Hey, Takumi, you won't believe what happened yesterday!

Takumi: What? What did I miss?

Haruto: There was a 1_____ during the second period!

Takumi: Wow! Was it serious?

Rena: It wasn't big, but there was a lot of 2_____.

Haruto: The 3_____ went off, and we had to 4_____ quickly through the emergency exits.

Takumi: Were you scared?

Rena: At first, yes. I felt 5_____ because some students were 6_____.

Haruto: Me too. But once we were outside, I felt 7_____.

Takumi: Did anyone get hurt?

Rena: No, thankfully. The teachers checked everyone at the 8_____ point, and then the fire 9_____ arrived.

Takumi: Oh, I'm glad. It must have been stressful, though.

Haruto: It was, but it's a good reminder to always be prepared and take 10_____ seriously.

B *Group work. Use the above dialogue as a model and make your own conversation about an emergency that can happen at your college.*

Presentation

Complete the short presentation paragraph by filling in your own information. Use new expressions you have learned. Memorize it!

The time I felt scared

There was one time when I was really scared. It happened _____いつ_____ ago.

I was at home/at school/outside/ ___緊急事態が発生した時、どこにいた___ on my own/ with my friends/ ___誰と___ when (suddenly) ___何が起こったか___.

I felt ___その時の感情___ because ___どうしてそう感じたのか___.

At that moment, I tried to think clearly about what to do. I remembered some of the safety drills, and I decided to call for help/ get to a safe place/ ___何をすると決めたのか___.

After a while, ___その後どうなったか___, and I felt a little more relieved. In the end, ___緊急事態がどのように終わったか___.

Luckily, I did not get hurt. / Unfortunately, I/my friend/ ___負傷した人___ got a(n) (small) injury and we had to go to the hospital.

It was a very frightening/stressful/dangerous situation. But I learned that in this kind of emergency, it's important to ___このような状況で何をすべきか、何を学んだ___.

Now, if something like this happens again, I feel prepared.

50

Self-Check

Let's see how well you understood the topic! Answer the following questions based on the chapter. If you are not sure, review the chapter.

1. What is the purpose of a safety drill?

2. What kinds of emergencies could happen at a technical college?

3. What does "duck, cover, and hold" mean, and when do you need to use it?

4. What should you do if the fire alarm goes off while you are in a classroom?

5. What are some items you should keep in an emergency kit?

6. Why is it important to practice safety drills regularly?

7. What do you think is the most important thing to remember during an emergency?

8. Why do technical colleges have safety drills for using chemicals and machines?

9. Where is the assembly point during an emergency in *your* college?

10. Can you describe the last safety drill you joined at *your* college?

CHAPTER ⑩
VACATIONS

- **Topic**: Talking about vacations and holiday activities
- **Interaction**: "Did you finish your summer homework?"
- **Presentation**: "My plans for the next vacation"

Warming Up

Listen and fill in the blanks. Then, write your own answers and practice asking and answering the questions with your partner. Track CIR_28

1. Which do you like better: summer or winter vacation?
   —I like _____ vacation better.
2. Do you prefer staying home or traveling during a long vacation?
   —I prefer _____ during a long vacation.
3. Are you more of a city traveler or a nature explorer?
   —I'm more of a _____ .
4. Do you finish your holiday assignments right away or at the end of the vacation?
   —I usually finish my assignments _____ .

> · be more of a [A]~
> 〜より[A]のようなタイプである，〜派
> · city traveler 都市旅行者
> · nature explorer 自然探検家
> · assignment 課題

Expressions

A *Practice each dialogue with your partner. Memorize new expressions.*

1. A: **Have you ever been abroad for a vacation?**
   B: Yes, I went to <u>Australia</u> during <u>spring break</u> <u>last year</u>. /
   No, I haven't, but I'd like to visit <u>New Zealand</u>.
2. A: **Do you have any plans for the next <u>summer break</u>?**
   B: Yes, I'm planning to <u>go camping with my friends</u>. /
   No, I haven't decided yet.
3. A: **How long is the <u>midterm break</u> at your college?**
   B: It's about a week. / We don't have a <u>midterm break</u>.
4. A: **What do you usually do during <u>study leave</u>?**
   B: I use it to <u>prepare for exams</u>. / I usually <u>just relax</u>.

> Vacation 休暇
> · **holidays and breaks** 学期中の休暇▶
> summer break 夏休み, winter break 冬休み, spring break 春休み, midterm break 中間休み, public holiday 祝日, long weekend 連休, short-term school holidays 学校行事後の短期休み, study leave 学習休暇, make-up holidays 振替休日
> · **activities** 休暇中にできること▶ travel 旅行する, go camping キャンプに行く, join the training camp 合宿に参加する, do club activities 部活動をする, play sports スポーツをする, work part-time アルバイトをする, visit relatives 親戚を訪ねる, study abroad 留学する, volunteer ボランティア活動をする, chill/relax at home 家でくつろぐ, join an internship インターンシップに参加する, spend time with friends 友達と過ごす

B *Replace the underlined words with your own variants and practice again.*

Reading

A *Listen to the audio while reading the text. Check the new words below.* Track CIR_29

📍 College vacations: active or relaxing?

In Japan, college students typically study for about 35 weeks each year. The academic year is divided into two semesters, with several long and short breaks in between for students to relax or explore new activities. The longest of these is the summer vacation.

During summer break, students have many activities to choose from. Some travel abroad to learn about new cultures and practice their language skills. Others join special training camps, called *gasshuku*, to focus on studying or learning new skills. Dedicated club members usually come to campus daily to practice with their teammates. Sophomores, juniors, and seniors often get part-time jobs to earn extra money.

A "staycation" ("stay" and "vacation") is a popular choice during shorter vacations or long weekends. It is a type of holiday where people stay home and enjoy local activities or nearby attractions within a day's reach.

However, not all students like super-active vacations. Some enjoy simply being a "couch potato"— watching their favorite TV shows, reading manga, or just relaxing at home.

How about you? Are you more of an active type or a couch potato?

---

typically (adv) 普通は，一般に
academic year (adj n) 学年度
semester (n) 学期
during (prep) 〜の間中ずっと
focus on (v prep) 〜に集中する
dedicated (adj) 熱心な
freshman (n) 大学・高専の1年生，新入生
sophomore (n) 大学・高専の2年生
junior (n) 大学・高専の3年生
senior (n) 大学・高専の4年生以上
earn (v) 稼ぐ
couch potato (n n) 家でゴロゴロする怠け者

※「**within**＋範囲＋**reach**」という構造は，「ある時間や距離の範囲内で到達できる」という意味を表す（例：within an hour's reach, within arm's reach）。

B *True or False. Find the evidence in the text.*

1. *Gasshuku* is a training camp that all students must attend. [TRUE / FALSE]
2. It is not unusual for upperclassmen to work part-time jobs. [TRUE / FALSE]
3. A "staycation" means traveling far from home for several days. [TRUE / FALSE]
4. A couch potato is someone who prefers passive leisure activities. [TRUE / FALSE]

Conversation

A *Listen to the conversation. Fill in the gaps with words you hear (find them in the word box below). Be careful! There are extra words in the word box.* Track CIR_30

club	classes	exciting	assignments	couch potato	holidays	travel
relaxing	practice	training camp	semester	break	active type	course
visit relatives	internship	stressful	study abroad	midterm	exercise

Did you finish your summer homework?

Misaki: I can't believe the new ₁_____ starts next week already.

Aika: Yeah, summer vacation went by so fast! What did you do this time?

Misaki: My family and I went to ₂_____. We stayed in another prefecture for several weeks. It was very ₃_____, but a bit boring. How about you?

Aika: I spent most of my time studying English because I want to ₄_____ next year. I also joined an English ₅_____ for extra practice. It was fun!

Misaki: Wow, you're definitely not a ₆_____! Hey, Kohei, did you finish your summer homework?

Kohei: Ah, not yet. I was so busy with baseball ₇_____ that I completely forgot about the ₈_____. Now, I'm trying to get them done at the last minute.

Aika: Oh no! That sounds ₉_____!

Kohei: Yeah, I need to plan my ₁₀_____ better next time. Baseball was great, but doing all this homework now is really tough!

B *Group work. Use the above dialogue as a model and make your own conversation about how you spent your summer or winter vacation.*

Presentation

Complete the short presentation paragraph by filling in your own information. Use new expressions you have learned. Memorize it!

My plans for the next vacation

I'm always really looking forward to _____ [楽しみにしている休日・休暇].

Last year, I _____ [去年のこの休暇に何をしたか] with _____ [誰と].

It was _____ [楽しかった、リラックスできた、退屈だった等].

Personally, I prefer active/relaxing vacations. So, this time, I'm planning to _____ [何をするつもりか]. I want to do this because _____ [理由].

If I have enough time, I might also _____ [もし時間に余裕があれば、どんな追加活動をしたいか]. But if my plans change, I can always _____ [もし当初の計画がキャンセルになったら（オプション１）] or _____ [もし当初の計画がキャンセルになったら（オプション２）].

I don't have college assignments. / I also have college assignments. I plan to finish them right away/at the end of the vacation so that I can _____ [このタイミングを選んだ理由].

I hope my vacation will be _____ [何を期待しているのか].

See you after the holidays!

Self-Check

Let's see how well you understood the topic! Answer the following questions based on the chapter. If you are not sure, review the chapter.

1. How do college students in Japan usually spend their summer break?

   _____.

2. What is a "staycation," and why do some people prefer it?

   _____.

3. What does it mean to be a "couch potato"?

   _____.

4. What is "gasshuku," and who can join it?

   _____.

5. How many weeks do you study and rest in *your* college? Is the balance good?

   _____.

6. Does *your* college offer any special programs or camps during the long holidays?

   _____.

7. Are there any club activities at *your* college during vacations? If yes, what kind?

   _____.

8. In your opinion, should students have assignments during vacations or just rest? Why?

   _____.

9. Does *your* college have midterm breaks? What do students usually do during them?

   _____.

10. What advice would you give to new students on how to make the most of their vacations?

    _____.

CHAPTER ⑪
VOLUNTEERING

- 📌 **Topic**: Helping society and the environment
- 📌 **Interaction**: "Come and help us clean the riverside!"
- 📌 **Presentation**: "How I want to make a difference"

Warming Up

Listen and fill in the blanks. Then, write your own answers and practice asking and answering the questions with your partner. **Track CIR_31**

1. Would you prefer to volunteer with children, animals, or the environment?
   —I would like to volunteer with _____.
2. Would you rather do creative or physical work as a volunteer?
   —I would prefer to do _____ volunteer work.
3. Is it more rewarding to see the results of volunteering or to enjoy the experience of helping others?
   —I think it is more rewarding to _____ of _____.
4. Would you rather volunteer alone or in a team?
   —I would rather volunteer _____.

- **environment** 環境
- **creative work** 創造的な仕事
- **physical work** 肉体労働
- **rewarding** やりがいがある

Expressions

A *Practice each dialogue with your partner. Memorize new expressions.*

1. A: **Have you ever done any volunteer work?**
   B: Yes, I have. I <u>participated in a tree-planting event</u>. /
   No, but I'd like to try <u>helping at an animal shelter</u>.
2. A: **What skills do you think volunteering can teach you?**
   B: It can teach skills like <u>teamwork</u> and <u>creative thinking</u>.
3. A: **If you could organize a volunteer project, what would it be?**
   B: I would organize <u>an event for the elderly</u>.
4. A: **What are the negative sides of volunteering?**
   B: It can <u>be emotional</u>. For example, <u>when you help people or animals</u>.

> Volunteering ボランティア活動
> ・**volunteer work** 活動▶ community clean-up 地域の清掃活動, animal shelter help 動物シェルターでの手伝い, teaching children 子供への教育, tree planting 植樹活動, food bank help フードバンクの支援, elderly care 高齢者の介護, event organization イベントの企画, collecting donations 寄付の収集
> ・**skills** スキル▶ communication コミュニケーション, teamwork チームワーク, leadership リーダーシップ, creative thinking 創造的な思考, problem-solving 問題解決, planning and organizing 計画と組織化
> ・**roles** 役割▶ organizer 企画者, helper 支援者, leader リーダー, cleaner 清掃者, fundraiser 資金集めの人

B *Replace the underlined words with your own variants and practice again.*

Reading

A *Listen to the audio while reading the text. Check the new words below.* Track CIR_32

Why volunteering is great for students

College life in Japan can be busy, but many students still make time to volunteer during vacations or holidays. Some colleges even have clubs for regular volunteer work.

Why do young people volunteer? Actually, volunteering benefits not only the people receiving help but also the volunteers themselves.

Volunteering can teach important life skills that are useful after college. It is different from typical school activities because it feels more like real work. Students learn to be responsible, work in a team, and follow directions. They can try different kinds of work, which can help them choose a future career. Keeping a record of volunteer work can also help students apply for jobs or internships later on.

Volunteering is also a good way to make new friends. Working with others who care about the same things makes students feel less lonely. It is also a good way to learn about other cultures and new ideas.

Finally, many people agree that volunteering is a rewarding experience. By cleaning parks, collecting donations, or visiting elderly people, students can make their town a better place. Seeing the results of your efforts can be very fulfilling.

Have you thought about joining a volunteer project?

---

   v   n
make time 時間を作る
  adj
regular 定期的な
 v
benefit 恩恵をもたらす
 v
receiving 受ける
   adj   prep
different from 〜とは違い
  adj
typical 一般的な
 n
record 記録
   v   prep
care about 〜に関心を持つ

 v
agree 同意する
   adj
rewarding やりがいのある
 n
effort 努力
   adj
fulfilling 充実感，充実した

※「**[A] feels more like [B]**」は、「AがよりBに近いと感じられる」という表現で、「more like」によって「より〜に近い」と比較を示す。
※「**have an impact on~**」は、「〜に影響を与える」、主語が対象に何らかの影響を及ぼすことを示す。

B *True or False. Find the evidence in the text.*

1. Volunteering is part of the college curriculum in Japan. [TRUE / FALSE]
2. Volunteering is only for people who want to work in social services. [TRUE / FALSE]
3. Volunteering can help students make friends with similar interests. [TRUE / FALSE]
4. One benefit of volunteering is seeing the positive results of your efforts. [TRUE / FALSE]

Conversation

A *Listen to the conversation. Fill in the gaps with words you hear (find them in the word box below). Be careful! There are extra words in the word box.* `Track CIR_33`

learning	record	food bank	teamwork	in groups	experience	list
helpers	collect	communication	gather	fulfilling	organization	history
clean-up	rewarding	leadership	community center	in pairs	planning

Come and help us clean the riverside!

Haruto: Hey, Rena, Misaki. What are you doing?

Misaki: Oh, hey, Haruto! We're putting up these posters to ₁_____ volunteers for a ₂_____ event. See?

Haruto: "Come and help us clean the riverside!" Hmm, sounds interesting. When is it happening?

Rena: It's this weekend, on Saturday morning. We'll meet at the ₃_____ and then clean the riverside ₄_____.

Misaki: You should come too!

Haruto: Saturday, huh? I don't know... I was planning to stay home and relax...

Rena: Come on, Haruto! It won't take long, and we really need more ₅_____.

Misaki: Yeah, and it's a great opportunity for you too. You said you want to improve your ₆_____ and ₇_____ skills, remember? This is a chance!

Rena: Plus, you can add it to your volunteer activity ₈_____. It's a win-win!

Haruto: Alright, I'll come. It sounds like it could be a ₉_____ ₁₀_____.

Misaki, Rena: Thanks for joining!

B *Group work. Use the above dialogue as a model and make your own conversation about a volunteer project you can join with your friends.*

Presentation

Complete the short presentation paragraph by filling in your own information. Use new expressions you have learned. Memorize it!

How I want to make a difference

I often/rarely take part in volunteering activities because _____[ボランティア活動に参加する・しない理由]_____.

In the past, I _____[過去のボランティア経験]_____ alone/ with _____[誰と]_____.

I/we _____[具体的に何をしたか1]_____ and _____[具体的に何をしたか2]_____. It was a very rewarding/fulfilling/challenging/fun/ _____[どのような経験だったか]_____ experience.

Recently, I have noticed a problem in my community/in the town where I live/on campus/ _____[場所]_____. The problem is that _____[具体的な問題]_____.

I think this is important because _____[この問題があなたや他の人にとってなぜ重要なのか]_____. I want to do something about it, so this time, I'm planning to _____[具体的な活動や目標]_____. I want to be a _____[役割]_____. I think it can also help me improve my _____[スキル1]_____ and _____[スキル2]_____ skills.

I hope my efforts will _____[そのボランティア活動により期待される成果]_____.

It might not solve the problem completely, but I hope I can make a difference with small steps.

Self-Check

Let's see how well you understood the topic! Answer the following questions based on the chapter. If you are not sure, review the chapter.

1. What are some common types of volunteer work mentioned in the chapter?
   _____.

2. What skills can students learn through volunteering?
   _____.

3. Why is volunteering often described as "rewarding"?
   _____.

4. How can volunteering help students prepare for their future careers?
   _____.

5. What are the benefits of volunteering with a group instead of alone?
   _____.

6. How does volunteering differ from regular school activities?
   _____.

7. What kind of volunteer activities do students at *your* college usually take part in?
   _____.

8. Are there any problems in *your* community that could be solved with volunteer work?
   _____.

9. Do you think volunteering is only for students with plenty of free time? Why or why not?
   _____.

10. What do you think about giving students extra exam points for volunteering as a reward?
    _____.

CHAPTER ⑫
CULTURAL EXCHANGE

📌 **Topic**: Talking about other cultures

📌 **Interaction**: "Exchange students are coming next semester"

📌 **Presentation**: "A tradition from my country I'd love to share"

Warming Up

Listen and fill in the blanks. Then, write your own answers and practice asking and answering the questions with your partner. Track CIR_34

1. Do you prefer learning about other cultures through cuisine, language, or history?
   —I prefer learning about other cultures through _____.
2. Would you rather host an exchange student or go abroad yourself?
   —I would rather _____.
3. Which is more interesting: learning about old traditions or modern culture?
   —I think learning about _____ is more interesting.
4. Where would you rather take your foreign friend first : to a themed café or a traditional tea ceremony?
   —I would rather take them to a _____ first.

- **cuisine** 料理
- **host** 迎える
- **exchange student** 交換留学生
- **abroad** 海外
- **foreign** 外国の
- **themed café** テーマカフェ

Expressions

A *Practice each dialogue with your partner. Memorize new expressions.*

1. **A: Does your college have any exchange programs?**
   B: Yes, we have a <u>homestay program</u>. / No, but <u>we have international days</u> to learn about other cultures.
2. **A: If you could live in another country for one year, where would it be?**
   B: I would live in <u>Canada</u> because <u>it has beautiful nature</u>.
3. **A: What do you think is the biggest challenge in intercultural communication?**
   B: I think <u>the language barrier</u> is the biggest challenge.
4. **A: Would you like to make international friends?**
   B: Yes, I'd love to. I enjoy <u>learning about different cultures</u>. / I'm not sure. <u>My language skills aren't very strong</u>.

International exchange　国際交流
- **activities and programs**　活動・プログラム▶ language learning　語学学習, cultural exchange　文化交流, cultural workshop　文化ワークショップ, homestay program　ホームステイ, school visit　学校訪問, project collaboration　共同プロジェクト
- **cultural understanding**　文化理解▶ customs　習慣, traditions　伝統, diversity　多様性, worldview　世界観, cultural norms　文化的規範, cross-cultural communication　異文化コミュニケーション
- **challenges**　問題点▶ language barrier　言葉の壁, miscommunication　誤伝達, unfamiliar customs　なじみのない習慣, stereotype　固定概念, culture shock　カルチャーショック

B *Replace the underlined words with your own variants and practice again.*

Reading

A *Listen to the audio while reading the text. Check the new words below.* `Track CIR_35`

📍 Can technology and culture be studied together?

Every year, many *kosen* students join exchange programs. They travel to other countries to study, experience different cultures, make new friends, and improve their language skills.

But even if you cannot travel abroad, there are still ways to gain international experiences in Japan. In 2023, a short-term program called KOSEN Global Camp was launched. Through this program, foreign students are invited to study and collaborate with their Japanese peers. The camp is held at different campuses across Japan and is done entirely in English.

At the camp, students join group projects, organize discussions, and work on hands-on activities. They improve their technical skills and learn to communicate with people from other cultures, building global connections. For example, in March 2023, one of the participating colleges in western Japan hosted around 30 students from Japan, Thailand, Singapore, Malaysia, and Vietnam. Together, they worked on a disaster prevention project while sharing and learning about each other's cultures.

These experiences help students grow and get ready for a global future—whether at home or abroad. What about you? Would you like to join a program like this or study abroad?

---

v
gain 得る
 adj
short-term 短期
 v   p.p.
was launched 開始された
 prep
through 〜を通じて
   p.p.   prep
be invited to 招待された
 n
peers 同僚
 prep
across 〜各地

adv
entirely 完全に，全て
 n
discussions ディスカッション
 adj
hands-on 実践的な

※「[A] is held at [B]」は、「AがBで開催される」という受動態の表現で、「is held」が過去分詞形、「at」で開催場所を示す。
※「whether [A] or [B]」は、「AでもBでも」、両方の可能性を含むことを示す。

B *True or False. Find the evidence in the text.*

1. The KOSEN Global Camp is only for Japanese students who want to study abroad. [TRUE / FALSE]
2. Participants in the camp are expected to communicate in English. [TRUE / FALSE]
3. The camp takes place in one specific location in Japan. [TRUE / FALSE]
4. The disaster prevention project included students from five different countries. [TRUE / FALSE]

Conversation

A *Listen to the conversation. Fill in the gaps with words you hear (find them in the word box below). Be careful! There are extra words in the word box.* Track CIR_36

living	at home	comfortable	studying	England	welcoming party	norms
customs	Canada	culture shock	host	collaboration	language barrier	homestay
foreign	abroad	miscommunication	cultural workshop	Australia	traditions

Exchange students are coming next semester

Aika: Hey guys, did you hear? Exchange students from 1_____ are coming next semester! We'll study together and even do a 2_____.

Takumi: That's so cool! I wonder if they'll feel any 3_____ when they get here. Our countries are so different. Do you think they'll enjoy Japanese food?

Rena: That's a good question. How about we organize a 4_____? We could cook some Japanese dishes and share our 5_____ and 6_____.

Aika: That sounds perfect! It should make them feel more 7_____.

Takumi: I like the idea, but I'm a bit worried about the 8_____. My English isn't very good.

Rena: Don't worry! This is a perfect chance for us to practice. And who knows? If it goes well, maybe we'll get to study 9_____ next year too.

Aika: That would be amazing! I've always wanted to try 10_____ in another country.

Takumi: Alright, let's start planning the party. It's going to be fun!

B *Group work. Use the above dialogue as a model and make your own conversation about welcoming exchange students at your college.*

Presentation

Complete the short presentation paragraph by filling in your own information. Use new expressions you have learned. Memorize it!

A tradition from my country I'd love to share

Today, I'd like to share a tradition from my country called _____[伝統の名称]_____.

This tradition is well-known/popular/unknown around the world. It is something we usually do every day/on special occasions/regularly/ _____[それが行われるのは]_____.

This tradition involves _____[活動、食べ物、習慣の簡単な説明]_____.

For example, people usually _____[具体的な詳細1]_____ and _____[具体的な詳細2]_____.

I think this tradition is special because _____[なぜこの伝統が大切なのか]_____. It's a great way to bring people together/celebrate history/show respect/keep culture alive/ _____[何をもたらすのか]_____.

If I could share this tradition with others, I would host an event/do a cultural workshop/ invite people to try it/ _____[どのように共有するか]_____. I believe this would help people learn more about _____[その国]_____ culture.

I hope to share _____[伝統の名称]_____ tradition with many people so they can enjoy it too.

Have you heard about it?

Self-Check

Let's see how well you understood the topic! Answer the following questions based on the chapter. If you are not sure, review the chapter to help you.

1. What are some examples of activities in cultural exchange programs?

   _____.

2. What is the main purpose of the KOSEN Global Camp?

   _____.

3. How can students benefit from joining cultural exchange programs?

   _____.

4. What challenges might students face during cultural exchange programs?

   _____.

5. What is "culture shock," and how can students deal with it?

   _____.

6. Why is cross-cultural communication important in today's world?

   _____.

7. Does *your* college offer any cultural exchange programs? If yes, what kind?

   _____.

8. What activities would you plan for exchange students visiting Japan for the first time?

   _____.

9. What do you think is the most important thing to learn about another culture?

   _____.

10. Do you think it's impossible to make international friends if your English skills are weak?

    _____.

TOEIC Bridge® リスニングテスト 1

Listening
This is the Listening test. There are four parts to this test.

● **Listening PART1** Track LT1_P1

Directions: You will see a set of four pictures in your test book, and you will hear one short phrase or sentence. Look at the set of pictures. Choose the picture that the phrase or sentence best describes.

1. Look at set number 1 in your test book.

(A)

(B)

(C)

(D)

Mark your answer. (A) (B) (C) (D)

● **Listening PART2** Track LT1_P2

Directions: You will hear some questions or statements. After each question or statement, you will hear four responses. Choose the best response to each question or statement.

2. Mark your answer. (A) (B) (C) (D)

3. Mark your answer. (A) (B) (C) (D)

4. Mark your answer. (A) (B) (C) (D)

5. Mark your answer. (A) (B) (C) (D)

6. Mark your answer. (A) (B) (C) (D)

7. Mark your answer. (A) (B) (C) (D)

● **Listening PART3** Track LT1_P3

Directions: You will hear some short conversations. You will hear and read two questions about each conversation. Each question has four answer choices. Choose the best answer to each question.

8. What are they talking about?
    (A) A new game
    (B) A new book
    (C) A new movie
    (D) A new restaurant

9. What does Jane think of the idea?
    (A) She doesn't know.
    (B) She likes it.
    (C) She isn't interested in it.
    (D) She is busy.

10. What is the woman going to do this afternoon?
    (A) Watch a movie
    (B) Play sports
    (C) Go shopping
    (D) Study

11. What subject does the man like?
    (A) English
    (B) Math
    (C) Science
    (D) History

● **Listening PART4** Track LT1_P4

Directions: You will hear some short talks. You will hear and read two questions about each talk. Each question has four answer choices. Choose the best answer to each question.

12. When will the tennis club have a practice match?
    (A) Next Monday
    (B) Next Wednesday
    (C) Next Thursday
    (D) Next Saturday

13. What should the members bring to the match?
    (A) Only a racket
    (B) Only a water bottle
    (C) Both a racket and a water bottle
    (D) Nothing

14. Where is the library located?
    (A) On the first floor
    (B) On the second floor
    (C) On the third floor
    (D) Outside the school

15. What can you do at the library?
    (A) Eat lunch
    (B) Have a break
    (C) Play sports
    (D) Borrow books

TOEIC Bridge® リスニングテスト 2

Listening
This is the Listening test. There are four parts to this test.

● **Listening PART1** Track LT2_P1

Directions: You will see a set of four pictures in your test book, and you will hear one short phrase or sentence. Look at the set of pictures. Choose the picture that the phrase or sentence best describes.

1. Look at set number 1 in your test book.

(A)

(B)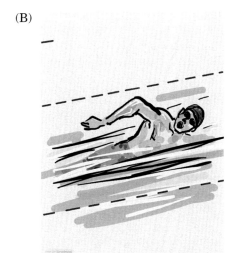

(C)

(D)

Mark your answer. (A) (B) (C) (D)

● **Listening PART2** Track LT2_P2

Directions: You will hear some questions or statements. After each question or statement, you will hear four responses. Choose the best response to each question or statement.

2. Mark your answer. (A) (B) (C) (D)

3. Mark your answer. (A) (B) (C) (D)

4. Mark your answer. (A) (B) (C) (D)

5. Mark your answer. (A) (B) (C) (D)

6. Mark your answer. (A) (B) (C) (D)

7. Mark your answer. (A) (B) (C) (D)

● **Listening PART3** Track LT2_P3

Directions: You will hear some short conversations. You will hear and read two questions about each conversation. Each question has four answer choices. Choose the best answer to each question.

8. Where does the woman work?
    (A) At a school
    (B) At a store
    (C) At a library
    (D) At a café

9. Why is the woman tired?
    (A) She studied hard.
    (B) She was sick.
    (C) She worked late.
    (D) She played sports.

10. What did the woman lose?
    (A) Her book
    (B) Her pen
    (C) Her phone
    (D) Her wallet

11. Where does the woman think she lost her pen?
    (A) At home
    (B) At school
    (C) At a store
    (D) At a park

● **Listening PART4** Track LT2_P4

Directions: You will hear some short talks. You will hear and read two questions about each talk. Each question has four answer choices. Choose the best answer to each question.

12. When will the school festival be held?
    (A) Next Thursday
    (B) Next Friday and Saturday
    (C) Next Sunday
    (D) Next month

13. What kind of food will be served at the food stall?
    (A) Only Japanese food
    (B) Only Western food
    (C) Various kinds of food
    (D) No food

14. What did the speaker lose?
    (A) A book
    (B) A pencil case
    (C) A coin case
    (D) A bag

15. What color is the pencil case?
    (A) Red
    (B) Blue
    (C) Yellow
    (D) Black

■編著者

Irina Ćošković（チョシュコヴィチ　イリーナ）　【執筆担当：CHAPTER 1 ~ 12】
現　　職：近畿大学工業高等専門学校 総合システム工学科 講師（英語）
最終学歴：関西大学大学院 文学研究科総合人文学専攻 博士課程後期課程
学　　位：博士（文学）
主　　著：Novoselova, I. (2021). "I Am Cone Sold Stober": Challenges of Translating the Humor of Diana Wynne Jones's Howl's Moving Castle into Japanese. *Invitation to Interpretation and Translation Studies*, 23, 23–46.

奈須　健（なす　けん）　【執筆担当：TOEIC Bridge® リスニングテスト】
現　　職：近畿大学工業高等専門学校 総合システム工学科 准教授（英語科主任）
最終学歴：大阪大学大学院 言語文化研究科言語文化専攻 博士後期課程単位取得退学
学　　位：修士（国際公共政策）
主　　著：杉田米行監修　佐藤晶子、山西敏博、竹休修一、奈須健 著『ボイス・オブ・アメリカ（VOA）ニュースで学ぶ英語 レベル2』（大学教育出版、2017年　共著）
　　　　　杉田米行編『第二次世界大戦の遺産―アメリカ合衆国』（大学教育出版、2015年　共著）
　　　　　杉田米行編『アメリカ社会への多面的アプローチ』（大学教育出版、2005年　共訳）

● 装丁協力：Marko Ćošković
● 本文デザイン：Irina Ćošković
● イラスト：Maro , 奈須ゆかり
● 音声録音・ポストプロダクション：Marko Ćošković, Irina Ćošković

CIRCUIT
―工業高等専門学校の学生のためのオーラル英語―

2025年4月10日　初版第1刷発行

■編 著 者 ── Irina Ćošković
　　　　　　　奈須　健
■発 行 者 ── 佐藤　守
■発 行 所 ── 株式会社 **大学教育出版**
　　　　　　〒700-0953　岡山市南区西市855-4
　　　　　　電話（086）244-1268㈹　FAX（086）246-0294
■印刷製本 ── ㈱大学教育出版

© Irina Ćošković and Ken Nasu 2025, Printed in Japan
検印省略　　落丁・乱丁本はお取り替えいたします。
本書のコピー・スキャン・デジタル化等の無断複製は、著作権法上での例外を除き禁じられています。本書を代行業者等の第三者に依頼してスキャンやデジタル化することは、たとえ個人や家庭内での利用でも著作権法違反です。
本書に関するご意見・ご感想を右記サイトまでお寄せください。

ISBN978-4-86692-354-3